CAMBRIDGE

Official Cambridge

Fun Skills

Home Booklet 1

Montse Watkin

Reading

Look at the colours and the letters. Write the names of the toys.

Hello. My name is
__ __ __ __ .

Hi. My name is
__ __ __ __ .

Hi. I'm
__ __ __ __ .

And I'm
__ __ __ __ __ __ .

Fun boost

Colour the robot. Use the code.

Reading

Read and colour the animals. Then write the animals on the grey farm.

On my farm, there are three sheep and two ducks.

On my farm, there are four sheep and a dog.

On my farm, there are two horses, two goats and a cat.

On my farm, there are ______________________________
____.

Fun boost

Match the animals with their footprints.

Reading

Follow the lines. Read and put a tick (✓) or a cross (✗).

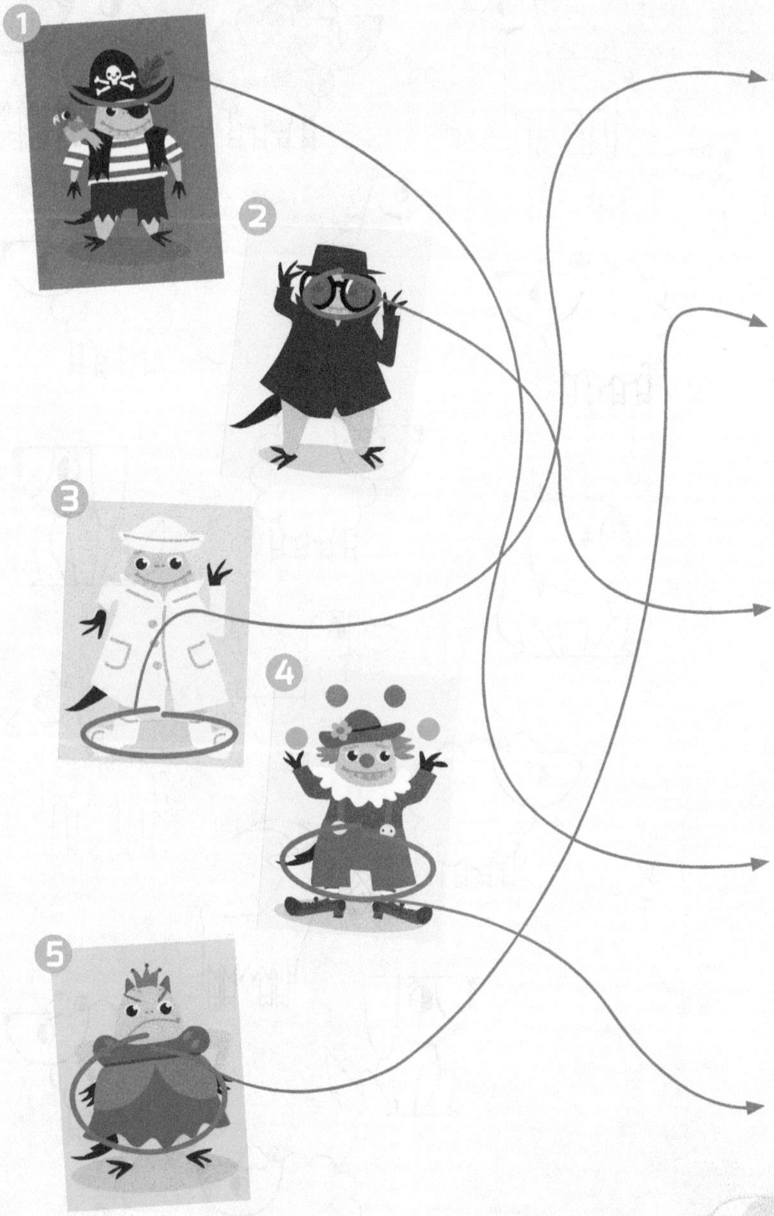

A These are boots. ☐

B This is a blue dress. ☐

C These are glasses. ☐

D This is a baseball cap. ☐

E These are shorts. ☐

Fun boost

Make a *Mix and Match* flip book.

1. Fold two sheets of A4 paper in half vertically.
2. Cut into three equal sections.
3. On each page, draw a head and a hat in the top section. Draw a body with clothes in the middle section. Draw legs and feet with shoes in the bottom section.
4. Mix and match the strips. Say what they are wearing.

Reading

Look and read. Answer *yes* or *no*.

1 There are two windows in the classroom.

yes no

2 Three children are sitting down.

yes no

3 There is a clock on the wall.

yes no

4 A girl is in front of a computer.

yes no

5 The door is open.

yes no

6 A boy is taking a book.

yes no

Fun boost

How many rulers and rubbers can you find?

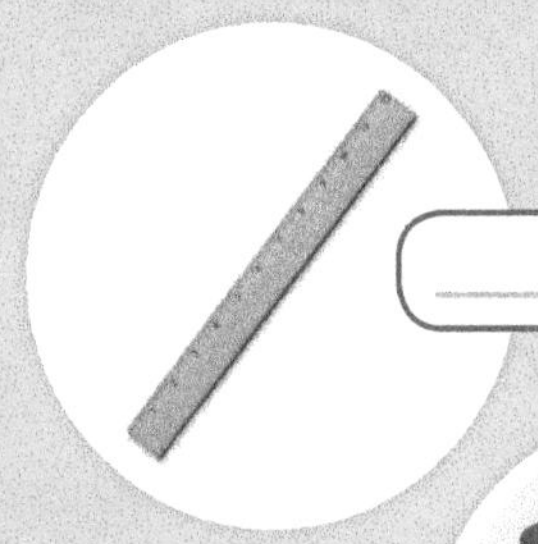

r	u	l	e	r	a	v	p	o
u	c	h	r	u	b	b	e	r
b	j	r	z	b	g	n	i	u
b	r	u	l	e	r	w	t	l
e	y	b	s	r	q	d	x	e
r	n	b	v	r	u	l	e	r
k	o	e	j	f	p	y	s	h
w	p	r	u	b	b	e	r	m

Reading

Read and complete the table.

Moyo's computer is on his desk and Kim's tablet is on her bookcase.

Kim's shoes are in the cupboard and Moyo's boots are on the bed.

Kim's crayons are on her desk and Moyo's pencils are on his bookcase.

Where is Moyo's baseball cap? His baseball cap is ...

Where is Kim's watch? Her watch is ...

	on the bed	in the cupboard	on the bookcase	on the desk
Kim				
Moyo				computer

Fun boost

mirror rug teddy bear sofa lamp

Draw the missing half. Then write the words.

1 ____________

2 ____________

3 ____________

4 ____________

5 ____________

Reading

Read and write the words.

One morning, an elephant sees an  owl in a tree.

'Hello, Owl. Oh, what small orange  **1** ________ you have.'

'Hello, Elephant. They're carrots.'

'And look, I can see some apple,' says Elephant.

'Yes, I have two apple  **2** ________ ,' says Owl, 'and my head

and  **3** ________ are bread.'

'You have very beautiful  **4** ________ too,' says Elephant.

'Thank you. They're bananas.'

'Mmmm. I love bananas for my breakfast!' says Elephant. 'I'm not your breakfast!' says Owl and he flies away.

Fun boost

Say the fruit on the plate and answer the questions. Then make your own fruit face.

On the plate, I can see pineapple, ...

Listening

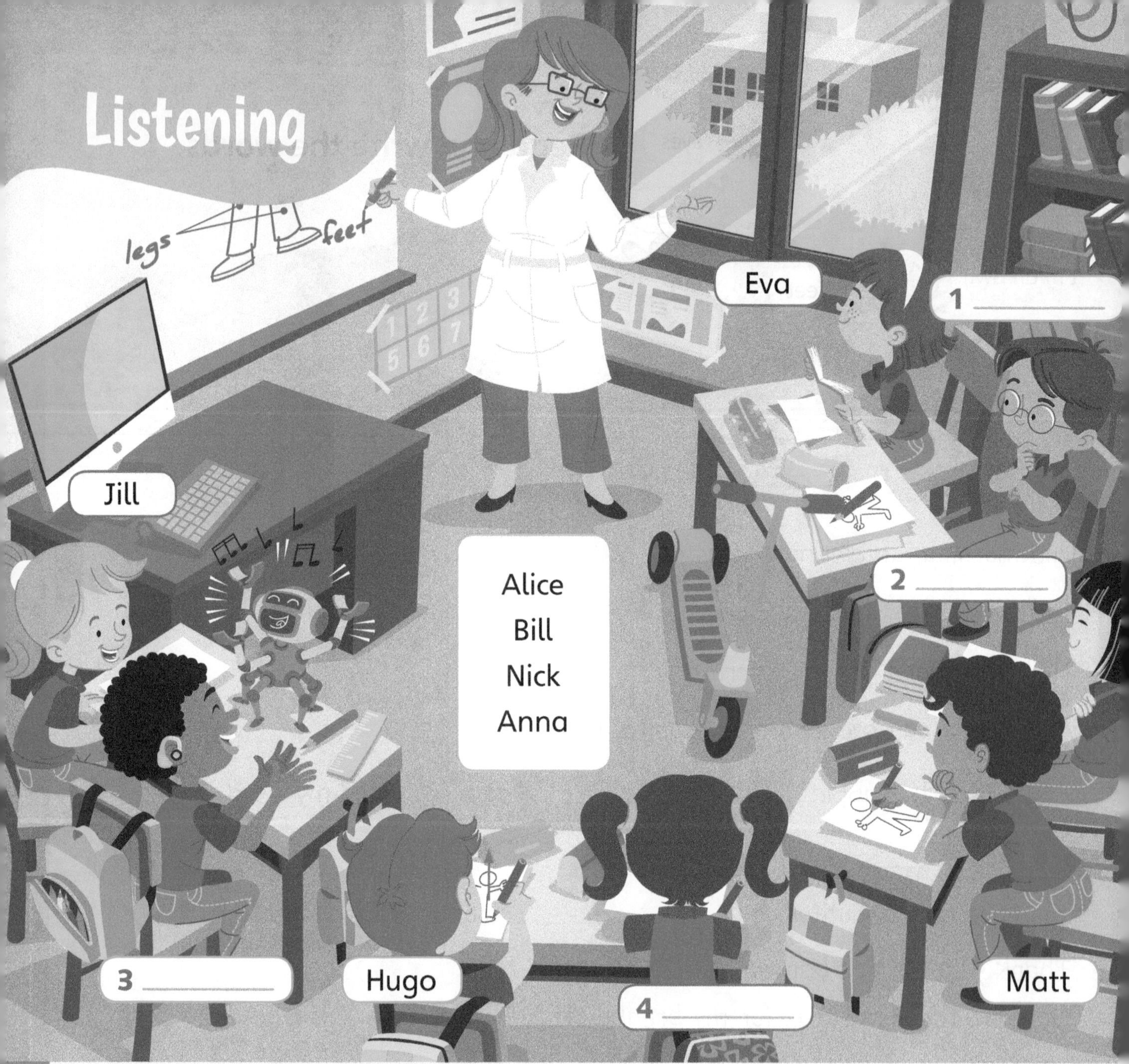

02 **Listen and write the names.**

Fun boost

Use the word *whiteboard* and write new words.

a colour r e d

a number _ _ _

an animal _ _ _ _

food _ _ _ _ _

where you sleep _ _ _

clothes _ _ _

Listening

03 **Listen and colour the squares. Then write numbers.**

classmates	1	2	3	4	5	6	7	8	9	10	11	12
badminton												
basketball												
football												
swimming												
tennis												

1 _____ children play badminton.

2 _____ children play basketball.

3 _____ children play football.

4 _____ children go swimming.

5 _____ children play tennis.

Fun boost

I can see number 1. It's green.

Find the numbers in the pictures. Point and say. Then draw a number in an object.

Listening

04 **Listen and tick (✓) the animals she photographs.**

Fun boost

Make a snake.

1 Draw circles onto a round paper plate.
2 Colour and decorate the lines like a snake.
3 Cut out along the lines to make a snake.
4 Give your snake a name.
5 Say the poem.

This is my snake.
It's long and thin.
It's got no legs
But it can swim!

Listening

05 **Listen and colour.**

Fun boost

Test your memory!

1 Look at the picture of Cool Park for two minutes.
2 Cover the picture of Cool Park.
3 Draw what you can remember.

Writing

Look and write the words.

hsoe nesaj kocs
tisrh sirtk

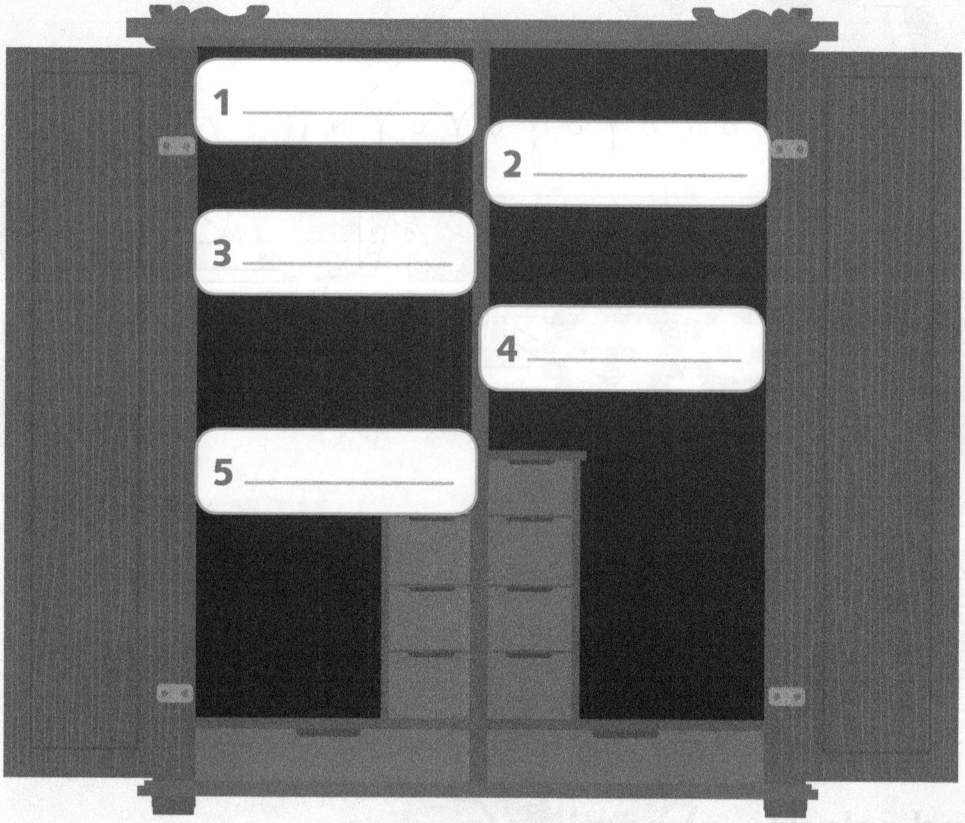

Fun boost

Practise your spelling.

1 Write a long word at the top of the paper.

2 Fold over and write the word again.
Fold and write the word again.
Fold and write the word again.

3 Open the paper. Count the words on your paper.

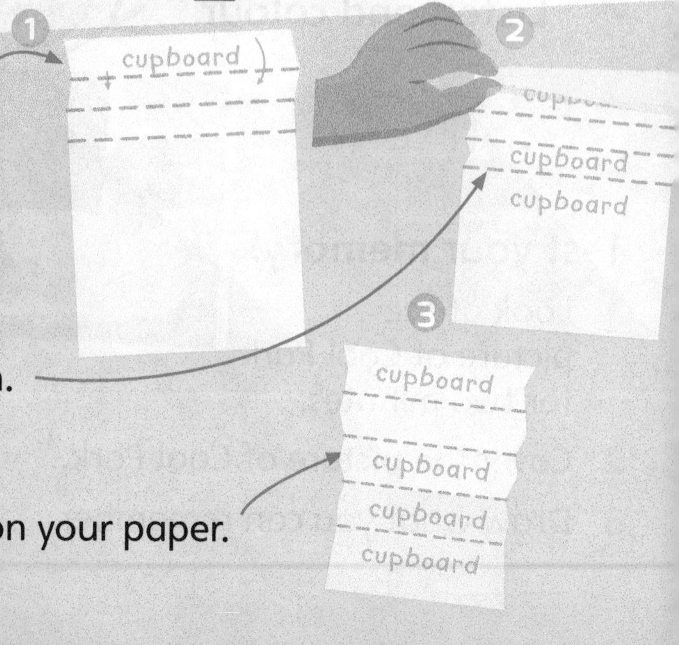

Writing

Look and write the words.

1 

2 

3 

4 

mm nn ll

a e i o u

5 

6 

7 

8 

Fun boost

Write invisible words.

1 Write words with a white crayon.
2 Paint over the words with watercolours.
3 Watch the magic! What can you see?

Writing

Look and write the words.

	House	Food	Toy	Animal
b	*bed*			
c		*carrots*		
l			*lorry*	
s				
t				*tiger*

~~bed~~ skateboard sheep ball
chair bat ~~lorry~~ lamp
sausage ~~carrots~~ ~~tiger~~
table lemon car teddy
tomato lizard sofa banana cat

Fun boost

Make fingerprint animals.

My fingerprint animal

Writing

Find and circle the words.
Write them in the correct place.

c	h	i	l	d	r	e	n
l	c	m	e	n	t	g	w
p	y	s	m	i	c	e	r
g	f	e	e	t	q	n	d
b	u	s	e	s	v	c	z
r	k	p	e	o	p	l	e
s	w	o	m	e	n	x	w
v	m	t	h	e	s	e	f

Singular  **Plural** 

1 → child → ________
2 → this → ________
3 → mouse → ________
4 → foot → ________
5 → man → ________
6 → woman → ________
7 → person → ________
8 → bus → ________

Fun boost

My feet

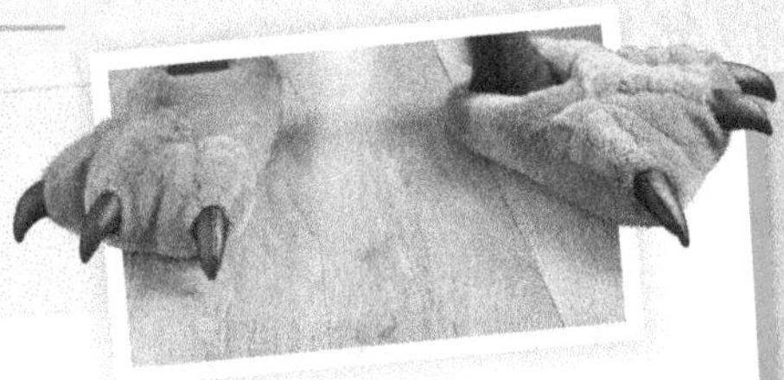

Draw and answer the questions.

1 Draw your feet. Are they big or small?
2 Colour your feet. Are they greenlike the picture?
3 Write your favourite places on your feet. Where do they take you?

Writing

Match the questions and answers. Write the missing information.

Marco	swimming	Beach Street	Sara	seven

1 What's your name?

2 What's your friend's name?

3 How old are you?

4 What's your favourite sport?

5 Where do you live?

A I'm ________ years old.

B In ________.

C His name's ________.

D It's ________.

E My name's ________.

Now answer the questions about YOU in your notebook.

Fun boost

Make a memory jar.

1 Find photos or draw pictures.
2 Write a sentence for each picture.
3 Put your memories in the jar.
4 Put it in a cupboard for two years!

My favourite animal is the elephant.

My best friends are David and Nina.

Writing

Read the questions. Match and colour the answers.

Are you ten years old?

Have you got a dog?

Can you fly?

Do you like the beach?

Is your favourite colour red?

Yes, it is.

No, I can't.

Yes, I do.

Yes, I am.

No, I haven't.

Fun boost

Invent a new you. Make an identity card.

1. Find a cool photo and a piece of card.
2. Stick the photo onto the card to make an ID card.
3. Write about the new you.
   - *How old are you?*
   - *Who are you?*
   - *What's your favourite colour?*
   - *What have you got?*
   - *What can you do?*

I'm **20** years old.
I'm a **pirate**.
My favourite colour is **red**.
I've got **three ships**.
I can **swim** with crocodiles!

Writing

Look and answer the questions. Then colour.

1 How many chairs are there in the dining room? ________
2 What is in front of the bookcase in the living room? a ________
3 What animal is in the bathroom? a ________
4 Where is the cat? in the ________
5 Is the tiger in the kitchen? ________
6 Who is on a bike? a ________

Fun boost

Look, read and write.

This is a house in a tree.
This is a house on a farm.
This is a house with a big light.
This is a house for dolls.
This is a house that is a boat.

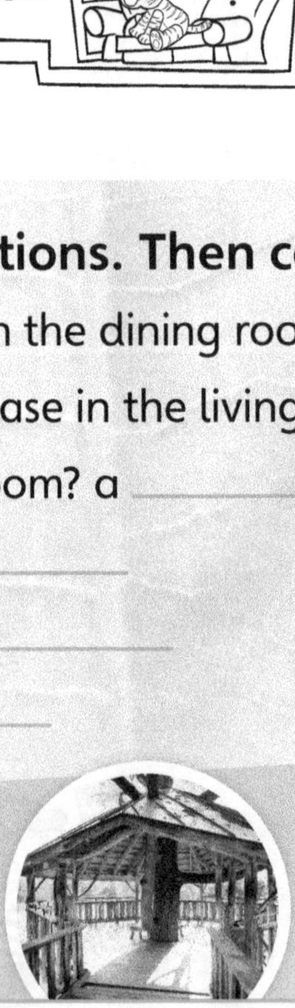

t*ree*________house

l________house

houseb________

Houses

d________house

f________house

Writing

Look at the pictures. Write one-word answers.

A

1

B

C

2

1A What can you see?

______

1B What is the lizard playing?
a ______

1C How many dogs are watching TV?

______

2A Where is the fish?
on the ______

2B What animal can play the piano?
a ______

2C Who is playing the violin?
a ______

Fun boost

Find six differences.

A

B

Speaking

1 Find and circle the objects in Picture A. Tick (✓) them when you find them.

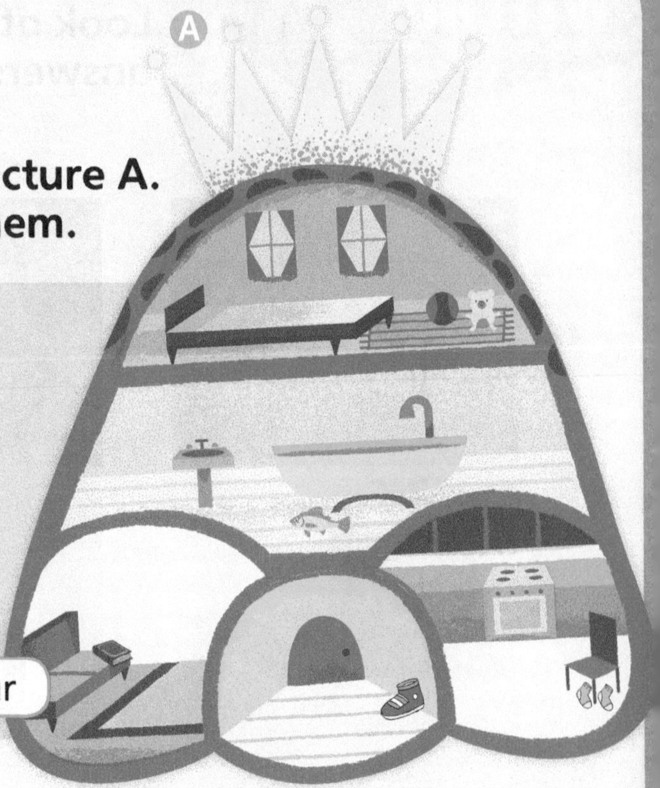

2 06 Listen and draw the objects in Picture B. Say where they are.

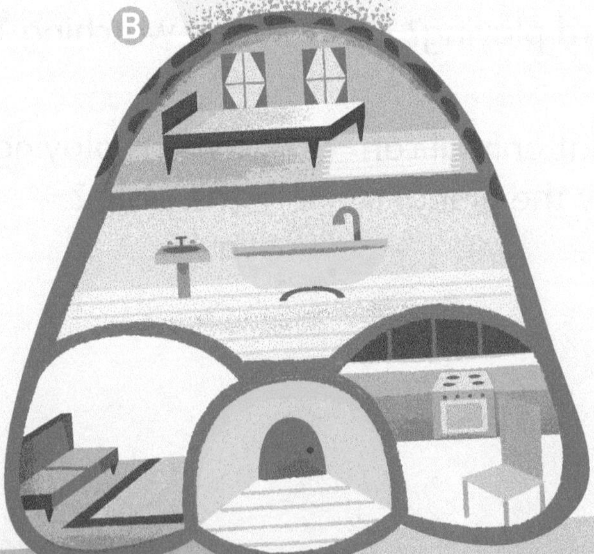

The ball is behind the sofa.

Fun boost

Make a pencil spinner.

1 Cut out two small circles.
2 Draw a fish.
3 Draw a bowl.
4 Put a pencil between the two circles.
5 Stick the circles together with the pencil in the middle.
6 Spin and see the fish in the fish bowl!

Speaking

1 07 **Look, listen and point.**

2 07 **Look at the photos again. Circle and say what you can see.**

green paint   map   yellow T-shirt   boat   big window   door
rainbows   happy girl   sad boy   game   book   guitar

Fun boost

Write an acrostic poem.

1 Write your name vertically. ↓
2 Think of words with the letters in your name.
3 Write the words across your name.
4 What words have you got?

leMonade
juice
kiwi
watEr

Elephant
Snake
Monkey
English

I'm Mike. I've got lemonade, juice, kiwi and water.

Speaking

❶ **Look and answer the questions.**

1 What's this? a __________
2 What's this? a __________
3 What's this? a __________
4 What's this? a __________

❷ 08 **Cut out the cards from page 31. Listen and put them in the correct place in the picture.**

Fun boost

Make a flying helicopter.

1 Cut a strip of paper.
2 Fold the paper
3 Put a paper clip on the end.
4 Fly your helicopter!

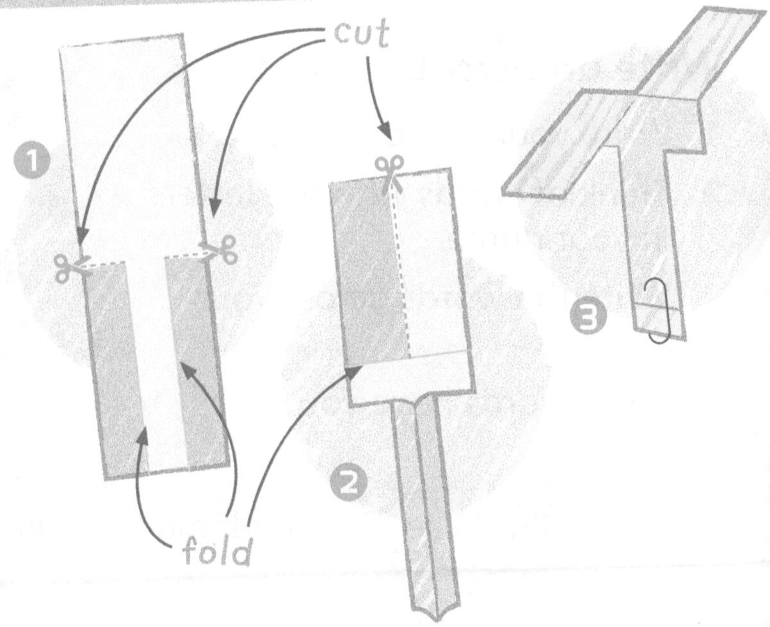

Speaking

09 **Listen, put your cards from page 31 on the squares and answer the questions.**

Fun boost

Find and count the objects. Write the number.

- [7] desks
- [ ] computers and keyboards
- [ ] ducks
- [ ] kites
- [ ] planes
- [ ] robots
- [ ] sheep
- [ ] ships

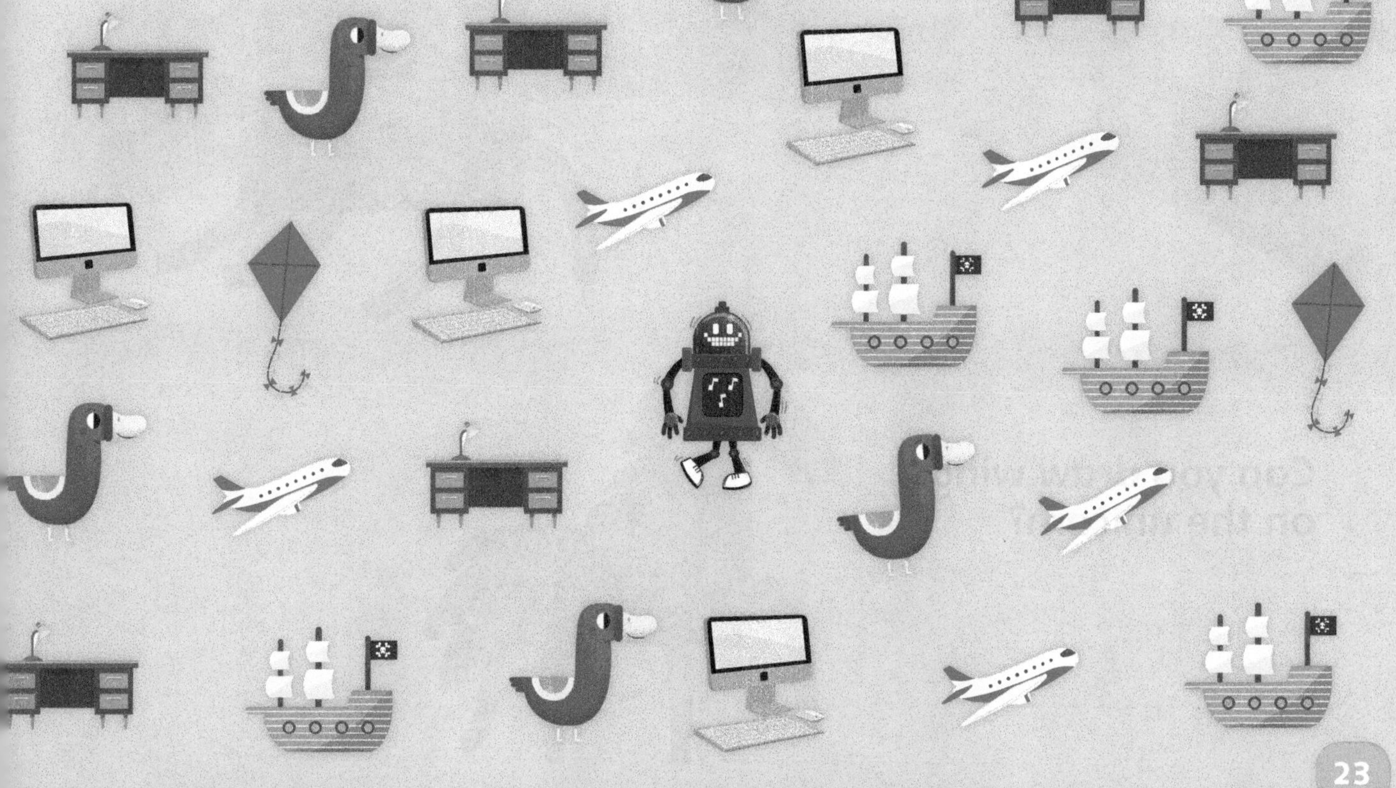

Jesse's unicorn

10 Jesse has got a pet. It's a unicorn.

One day, Jesse's unicorn is sad.

'All my friends can fly,' he says.

'I can help you,' says Jesse. 'We can fly together with my wings.'

Now Jesse's unicorn is happy.
And they fly to school every day.

Can you draw wings on the unicorn?

Captain Zoom

Every day … I ZOOM, ZOOM, ZOOM on my bike in the morning …

… and on my boat in the afternoon …

… on my skateboard in the evening …

… and on my plane to that yellow moon!

Sometimes I zoom into a tree … ouch!

So now I wear protection, you see.

Zooming is … COOL!

What do you wear to protect your head?

Bobbie's rainbow

12 Bobbie loves painting. One day, he sees a grey rainbow.

He has an idea. He puts his paints in his toy plane.

He flies his plane up and up … and … whoosh!

The plane throws the colours onto the rainbow …

… and onto Bobbie, too!

Now Bobbie is a rainbow boy!

What colour are you today?

I'm ____________.

Nedda, the space girl

13 Nedda lives on the moon.
She loves sport.

She plays basketball with her robot …

… and football with the moon monster.

She can't fly, but she rides her space bike around the moon.

Her favourite sport is swimming between the stars.

One day, she wants to play tennis with Martin from Mars!

Can you write six ball games?

1 ____________________ 4 ____________________

2 ____________________ 5 ____________________

3 ____________________ 6 ____________________

Piper – am I a bat?

14 I'm not a bird, but I can fly.

I'm not an alien, but I've got three eyes.

I'm not an octopus, but I've got pink arms.

I'm not a monster, but I've got five horns.

What am I?

Yes! I'm a …

funny,

silly

bat!

Can you see bats in the morning, in the afternoon or at night?

I can see bats in the ______________________ .

Detective Leon

Can you see me? It's me, Leon. I am a detective!

I like looking …

… and listening.

I find all the things you can't find.

I can find your school books …

… your favourite toys …

… your pets in the park …

… your snacks and sweets …

… and your grandparents too!

Here is my card!

What can Leon find for you? Write and draw.

Frankie's magic bag

Frankie loves having fun at the weekend. She takes her cool orange bag too!

At the park, Frankie takes out of her bag …

… an orange skateboard. Nice!

At the beach, Frankie takes out …

… an orange boat and an ice-cream. Great!

At her friend's party, Frankie takes out …

… an orange piano to play *Happy Birthday!* Wow!

And when she waves goodbye, she takes out …

… an orange kite and flies away. Bye!

Imagine this is your magic bag. Draw one thing inside.

Object cards

Cambridge University Press
www.cambridge.org/elt

Cambridge Assessment English
www.cambridgeenglish.org

Information on this title:
www.cambridge.org/9781108582148

First published 2020

20 19 18 17 16 15 14 13 12 11 10 9 8

Printed in Great Britain by Ashford Colour Press Ltd.

A catalogue record for this publication is available from the British Library

ISBN 978-1-108-58214-8 Student's Book and Home Booklet with Online Activities

Author acknowledgements

The author would like to thank the marvellous CUP editing team for their expertise and to Matthew, Ata and mum for everything else.

Publisher acknowledgements

The authors and publishers are grateful to Robert Hill for reviewing the content and style of the stories.

Acknowledgements

The authors and publishers acknowledge the following sources of copyright material and are grateful for the permissions granted. While every effort has been made, it has not always been possible to identify the sources of all the material used, or to trace all copyright holders. If any omissions are brought to our notice, we will be happy to include the appropriate acknowledgements on reprinting and in the next update to the digital edition, as applicable.

Key: BG = Background

Photography

The following photographs are sourced from Getty Images.

BG: Chris Clor; Mima Foto/EyeEm; Marka/Universal Images Group; Elisabeth David/EyeEm; **Reading:** sitox/E+; Dorling Kindersley; John Kroetch; Nikiteev_Konstantin/iStock/Getty Images Plus; gyener/DigitalVision Vectors; bamlou/DigitalVision Vectors; DNY59/E+; ayala_studio/E+; Cultura RM Exclusive/Christine Schneider; FG Trade/E+; Dash_med/iStock/Getty Images Plus; a_namenko/iStock/Getty Images Plus; **Listening:** Rivers Dale/Image Source; PeopleImages/iStock/Getty Images Plus; **Writing:** FatCamera/E+; Pollyana FMS; PeopleImages/E+; Sollina Images; Santiago Urquijo/Moment; Paul Blackley/Moment; Shoji Fujita/DigitalVision; Anadolu Agency; Elva Etienne/Moment; Ridofranz/iStock/Getty Images Plus; BJI/Blue Jean Images; MCT/Tribune News Service; Michael H/DigitalVision; RichVintage/E+; Jose Luis Pelaez Inc/Digital Vision; Andy Crawford/Dorling Kindersley; Andia/Universal Images Group; Jon Bower at Apexphotos/Moment Open; Hoxton/Tom Merton; Christian Peters/iStock/Getty Images Plus; Barry Miller/EyeEm; Hendrata Yoga Surya/EyeEm; Manabu Ogasawara/Stockbyte; Carol Yepes/Moment; Donald Iain Smith/Photodisc; Speaking: PeopleImages/E+; Michael H/DigitalVision; ArtMarie/E+; Colorblind Images LLC/DigitalVision; Milan_Jovic/E+; Westend61; **Captain Zoom:** sturti/E+; Sollina Images; **Bobbie's rainbow:** PeopleImages/E+; **Nedda, the space girl 27:** John Kroetch; **Piper – am I a bat?:** sitox/E+; **Object cards:** John Kroetch; George Coppock/Photolibrary; Dorling Kindersley; Peter Dazeley/Photographer's Choice; Tetra Images.

The following photograph are sourced from other libraries/sources.

Writing: Copyright © http://www.trueaimeducation.com. Reproduced with kind permission of Janine LaTulipee; **Speaking:** wonderlandstock/Alamy Stock Photo.

Front cover photography and illustrations by Collaborate Agency; Amanda Enright; Leo Trinidad; Jhonny Nunez; Pol Cunyat; Benedetta Capriotti; Dan Widdowson; P and P Studio/Shuterstock; Piotr Urakau/Shuterstock.

Illustrations

Collaborate Agency; Fran and David Brylewska - Beehive; Amanda Enright - Advocate Art; Dave Williams - Bright Agency; Pablo Gallego - Beehive; Leo Trinidad - Bright Agency; Wild Apple Design.

Audio

Audio Production by DN and AE Strauss Ltd, with engineer Mike Dentith, and additional skills tasks by Ian Harker.

Design

Design and typeset by Wild Apple Design Ltd
Cover design by Collaborate agency.